LOTS TO SPOT

OUT AND ABOUT

by Genie Espinosa

WINDMILL
BOOKS

Published in 2020 by Windmill Books, an imprint of Rosen Publishing
29 East 21st Street, New York, NY 10010

Illustrations: Genie Espinosa
Text: Paul Virr
Editors: Samantha Hilton and Joe Harris

Cataloging-in-Publication Data

Names: Espinosa, Genie.
Title: Out and about / Genie Espinosa.
Description: New York : Windmill Books, 2020.
| Series: Lots to spot
Identifiers: ISBN 9781538391648 (pbk.)
| ISBN 9781538391662 (library bound) | ISBN 9781538391655 (6 pack)
Subjects: LCSH: Picture puzzles–Juvenile literature.
Classification: LCC GV1507.P47 E875 2020 | DDC 793.73–dc23

Manufactured in the United States of America

CPSIA Compliance Information: Batch #BS19WM:
For Further Information contact Rosen Publishing,
New York, New York at 1-800-237-9932

CONTENTS

Step inside a world of awesome puzzles!

For some, you need to spot the differences between two pictures. For others, you need to find the odd one out. You'll find all the answers at the back of the book. Turn the page to get started!

FUN AND GAMES

Step right up! Ride the roller coaster, then find 10 differences to win a prize!

COOKING UP A STORM

Which of the chefs is armed with both a spoon and a saucepan?

UNDER LOCK AND KEY

Each key opens a lock with matching decorations.
Which lock cannot be opened?

CANDY
STORE

Everything here looks yummy! Can you spot 10 differences between these sweet-toothed scenes?

OUT OF TUNE

A member of the choir didn't read the dress code properly. Who has gotten it a little bit wrong?

MODERN ART

Which of the forgeries has a mistake on it?

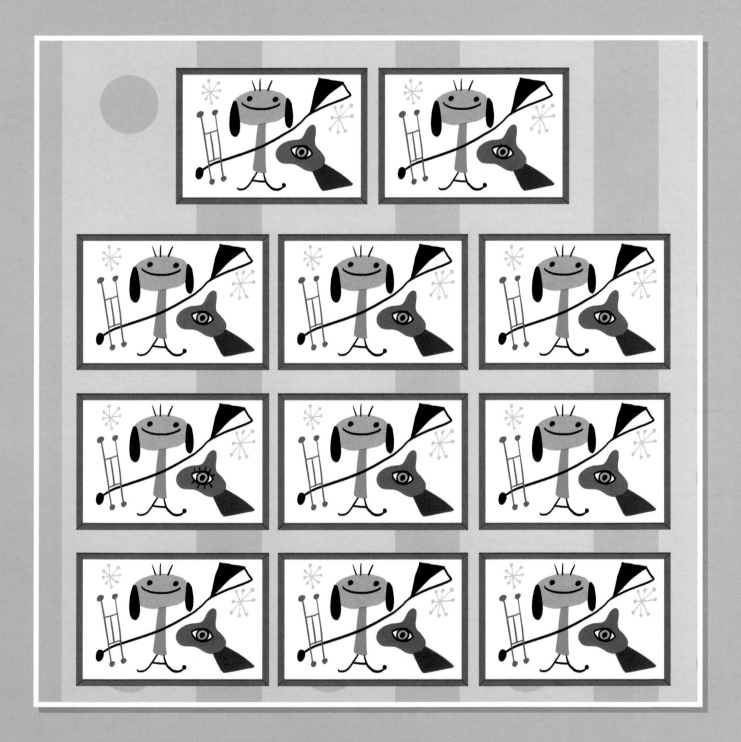

AT THE MALL

Get ready to shop and spot down at the mall.
Can you find 10 differences?

FLYING THE FLAG

Only one of these flags features an odd number of stars. Can you find it?

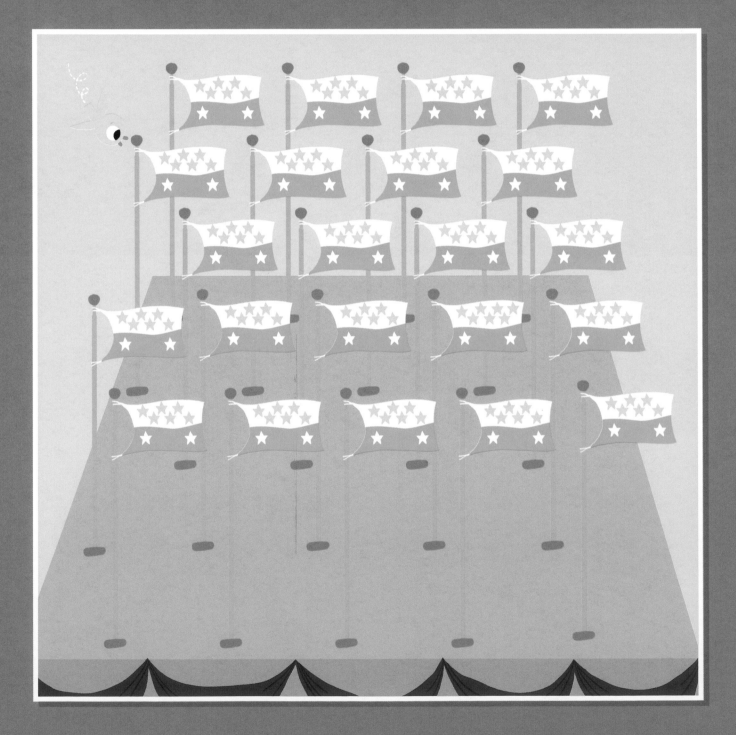

KEEP ON RUNNING

Which of the athletes is running solo, rather than with other club members in matching tops?

MAGIC
SHOW

Abracadabra! See if you can conjure up 10 differences between these magic show scenes.

OUT OF STEP

Which dancer is a move behind the others?

REALLY ROYAL

Begging your pardon, your Highness, but one of these pictures is not quite the same. Which one is it?

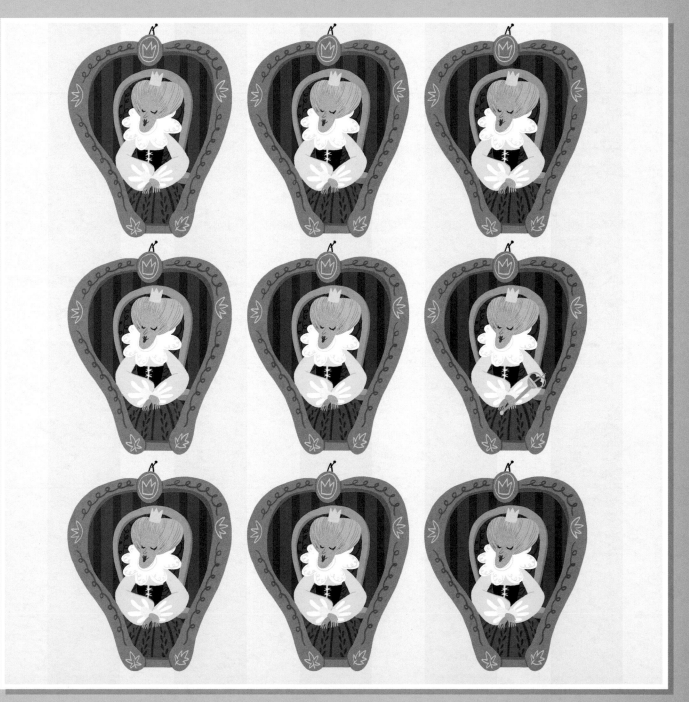

CRAZY KITCHEN

Slice, dice, and spot 10 differences in the kitchen!

FLYING HIGH

Search the sky for 10 differences
between these scenes.

JOIN THE CIRCUS!

The circus is in town! Which of the shadow outlines is not an exact match for the performer?

BABOON ON A BIKE

A baboon riding a bike! How else would he get to school? Which outline doesn't match the baboon in the middle?

HAPPY NEW YEAR!

It's party time! Can you spot 10 differences between these Chinese New Year scenes?

TIME FOR TEA

Spot 10 differences between
these tea party scenes.

FANCY THAT!

Which of Madame Chapeau's fancy hats does not feature in the pages of her magazine?

I SPY

Can you spot the one fruit that is different from the rest?

NIGHT NIGHT

Which of the houses has all of its lights switched off, ready for bed?

ANSWERS

Page 4-5 Fun and Games

Page 6 Cooking Up a Storm

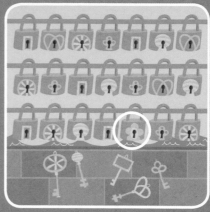

Page 7 Under Lock and Key

Page 8-9 Candy Store

Page 10 Out of Tune

Page 11 Modern Art

Page 12-13 At the Mall

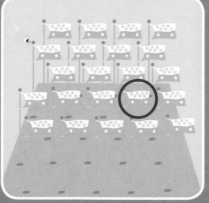

Page 14 Flying the Flag

Page 15 Keep on Running

Page 16-17 Magic Show

Page 18 Out of Step

Page 19 Really Royal

Page 20 Crazy Kitchen

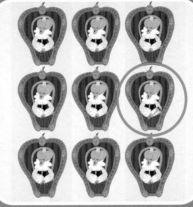

Page 21 Flying High

Page 22 Join the Circus!

Page 23 Baboon on a Bike

Page 24-25 Happy New Year!

Page 26 Time for Tea

Page 27 Fancy That!

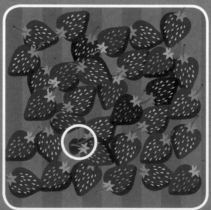

Page 28 I Spy

Page 29 Night Night